Thank You, Money:

Affirmations and Visualization techniques to Heal and Harmonize Your Relationship with Money

By Sapphire Celestina

Copyright

Thank You, Money: Affirmations and Visualization techniques to Heal and Harmonize Your Relationship with Money

Copyright © [2024] by Sapphire Celestina

All rights reserved.

No part of this book may be reproduced, distributed, or transmitted in any form or by any means, including photocopying, recording, or other electronic or mechanical methods, without the prior written permission of the author, except in the case of brief quotations embodied in critical reviews and certain other non-commercial uses permitted by copyright law. For permission requests, please contact the author at the address below.

This book is a work of nonfiction, created with the support of ChatGPT. The author has made every effort to ensure the accuracy of the information provided at the time of publication. However, neither the author nor the publisher makes any representations or warranties regarding the completeness or accuracy of the content, and they disclaim any implied warranties of merchantability or fitness for a specific purpose. The advice and strategies presented in this book may not be appropriate for all situations. Readers are encouraged to consult with professionals where needed.

Published by Amazon Kindle Direct Publishing (KDP)

Imprint: Independently published

Cover design by Sapphire Celestina, with photography sourced from Pexels.

ISBN: 9798342295345

Table of Contents

How to Use This Book..3-5

Introduction..6-7

The Affirmations..8-51

Visualization Techniques..52-87

Conclusion..88-89

About the Author..90

Other Works by Sapphire Celestina..91

How to Use This Book

This book is your guide to transforming any limiting beliefs, financial anxieties, or emotional barriers that may be holding you back from experiencing true abundance and peace.

To get the most out of this book, here's how you can approach it:

Read with an Open Mind

Each section is crafted to gently guide you through different aspects of financial healing. Begin by reading through the book at your own pace, allowing the words to resonate with your current feelings about money. Approach the affirmations and visualizations with openness, even if they feel unfamiliar at first.

Set Intentions

Before diving into the affirmations, take a moment to set a clear intention. Whether it's to release financial stress, invite more abundance, or simply feel more at ease with money, knowing your intention will help focus your energy and attention as you move through the practices.

Engage with the Affirmations

Affirmations are meant to be repeated consistently. As you read through each chapter, feel free to either speak the affirmations aloud or write them down. The key is to engage with them regularly—morning, evening, or whenever you feel called. Repetition builds new beliefs and habits, so allow yourself to revisit your favorite affirmations frequently.

Incorporate Visualization Techniques

Alongside the affirmations, you'll find guided visualization exercises. These techniques will help you envision the financial abundance you seek, and they serve as powerful tools to shift your mindset. You don't need to do them all at once—choose the ones that resonate with you and incorporate them into your daily or weekly routine.

Reflect on Your Progress

As you move through the book, take time to pause and reflect. Journaling can be a helpful way to track your thoughts, emotions, and progress. Consider noting how your relationship with money evolves as you continue practicing the affirmations and visualizations.

Personalize Your Practice

Not every affirmation or visualization will resonate the same way with everyone, and that's okay! Feel free to personalize the practices, adjusting the words or visualizations to fit your specific financial goals and emotional needs. The more aligned these tools are with your unique journey, the more effective they will be.

Be Patient with Yourself

Healing your relationship with money is a process, and it takes time. Approach this journey with self-compassion. There's no rush, and each step forward is progress, no matter how small. The key is consistency and trust in the process.

Thank You, Money is more than just a collection of affirmations—it's a healing journey. Use this book as a daily companion, returning to it whenever you need a reminder to invite peace, gratitude, and abundance into your financial life. The more you practice, the more you'll begin to see the flow of money shift toward ease and harmony.

Introduction

Welcome to *Thank You, Money: Affirmations and Visualization techniques to Heal and Harmonize Your Relationship with Money*. This book is an invitation to transform the way you think about and interact with money. For many of us, money has been a source of tension, fear, or even guilt. Whether from past experiences, societal expectations, or inherited beliefs, our relationship with money can often feel strained. This book offers a path to healing that relationship and bringing it into harmony with who you are today.

The affirmations within these pages are designed to help you create a respectful, wise, and peaceful connection with money—one rooted in gratitude and understanding. They will guide you in letting go of limiting beliefs, releasing financial anxieties, and embracing a new, harmonious mindset toward wealth. By practicing these affirmations, you'll begin to see money not as something to fear or avoid but as a supportive presence in your life, one that helps you achieve your goals and live your purpose.

This book isn't about chasing after wealth for its own sake. It's about learning to appreciate and honor money as a natural flow of energy in your life, one that can serve you when treated with care and respect. As you heal and harmonize your relationship with money, you'll find yourself open to new opportunities, more peaceful in your financial decisions, and more connected to the abundance that is available to you.

In addition to the affirmations, you'll find visualization techniques to deepen your healing journey. These practices will help you tap into the energy of abundance, invite higher truths about wealth, and heal not only your present self but also any past or inherited financial wounds.

As you embark on this journey, remember that healing takes time, patience, and self-compassion. Be kind to yourself as you work through any past money blocks, and trust that you are on the path to creating a balanced, peaceful, and abundant financial life.

Let's begin this journey of healing, gratitude, and transformation together.

The Affirmations

1. "I honor and respect the energy of money, recognizing it as a tool for positive change and growth in my life."

2. "I release any past negativity I have held towards money and embrace it as a reflection of abundance and generosity."

3. "Money is a form of energy that flows to me easily and supports my highest good."

4. "You support my growth, money, and I'm grateful for the expansion you allow me to experience."

5. "I welcome money into my life with gratitude, knowing it allows me to serve and uplift others."

6. "I trust in my ability to attract and manage wealth with wisdom and responsibility."

7. "Thank you, money, for helping me achieve my financial goals with ease and grace."

8. "Money, I no longer fear your absence—I believe you are always nearby, ready to flow in."

9. "I appreciate all the ways money has made my life richer and more fulfilling."

10. "Thank you, money, for supporting me in moments of transition and change."

11. "While happiness is not dependent on money, it enhances my ability to pursue a life I love."

12. "I forgive myself for any past misunderstandings about money and open myself to a new, positive relationship with it."

13. "I am deserving of financial abundance, and I use money wisely to create a fulfilling and meaningful life."

14. "I respect money as a resource that can be used for good, and I align my financial actions with my values."

15. "I cultivate a mindset of abundance, knowing that wealth is a natural part of the infinite possibilities available to me."

16. "Money, I no longer see you as distant—you're a natural part of my everyday experience."

17. "You've always had my back, money, and I trust that you'll continue supporting me as I move forward."

18. "I recognize the value of money as a tool that requires thoughtful management and respect."

19. "I approach money with maturity and responsibility, understanding its role in creating stability and security."

20. "I treat money with care, knowing that it reflects the energy and effort I invest into my life."

21. "I honor the presence of you in my life, money, and use you to create balance."

22. "I respect the flow of money, allowing it to be a means of exchange for the things that matter most in life."

23. "I am mindful of the decisions I make regarding money, always striving for balance and thoughtful stewardship."

24. "Money, when handled wisely, contributes to my well-being and the well-being of others."

25. "I respect the value of money and make decisions that reflect my appreciation for its role in my life."

26. "I understand that financial growth comes with patience, planning, and disciplined choices."

27. "Money, I see you as a bridge to new horizons, helping me expand beyond my limits."

28. "I see money as a resource to be respected, knowing that its worth lies not in accumulation but in the mindful way it is used."

29. "Thank you, money, for helping me take care of myself and the people I love."

30. "Money, you make it possible for me to live a life of freedom, and I'm so thankful for that."

31. "I release the negativity I once held towards money and embrace it with kindness and respect."

32. "Money, I see now that our relationship can be one of lightness, not just seriousness."

33. "I apologize to money for the ways I have disrespected it in the past, and I now welcome it with gratitude."

34. "Money, you've made it possible for me to live the life I want, and I'm grateful for every moment you've been there."

35. "I choose to see money as a positive force in my life, treating it with the respect it deserves."

36. "I trust you completely, money, and I know you'll always show up at the right time."

37. "I am thankful for all the moments money has given me peace of mind."

38. "Thank you, money, for always showing up when I've needed you most."

39. "I am grateful for the times money has helped me take care of myself and my loved ones."

40. "Thank you, money, for being a steady presence in my life, always supporting my growth."

41. "I appreciate how money has helped me pursue my dreams and goals."

42. "I'm ready to let go of past conflicts and work with you, money, in a spirit of partnership."

43. "Thank you, money, for providing me with the resources to enjoy life's pleasures."

44. "I am grateful for the times money has allowed me to explore new opportunities."

45. "I shift my mindset from criticism to respect, understanding that money is a valuable resource when used with intention."

46. "I recognize the ways I have spoken poorly of money and now choose to speak of it with maturity and gratitude."

47. "Money, you bring me peace and security, and I'm so grateful for your presence in my life."

48. "I let go of any negative energy I have directed towards money, opening myself to a healthier, more respectful relationship."

49. "I understand that money is neither good nor bad—it is my perspective that shapes its impact, and I now choose a balanced, respectful view."

50. "I embrace a new chapter with money, one grounded in respect, maturity, and thoughtful stewardship."

51. "Money, you're like that friend who always has my back, and I appreciate you so much."

52. "Money, I'm opening the door for you to enter in ways that feel effortless and aligned with my values."

53. "I release the judgments I've held about money and choose to honor its value in my life."

54. "Thank you, money, for always being there to help me take care of myself."

55. "I acknowledge the harm I've caused by undervaluing money and now commit to a respectful partnership with it."

56. "I forgive myself for any harsh views I've held about money and choose to embrace it with a fresh, positive perspective."

57. "I accept money as a valuable resource and treat it with the respect it deserves moving forward."

58. "You don't have to feel distant, money—I'm allowing you to be present without needing to control your flow."

59. "I shift from seeing money as a source of frustration to recognizing it as a means of creating growth and opportunities."

60. "I am grateful for the lessons money has taught me and now choose to engage with it thoughtfully and respectfully."

61. "Thank you, money, for supporting my journey and helping me create the life I want."

62. "Money, I am open to discovering the ways you can enhance my relationships and connections."

63. "I appreciate the presence of money in my life and the support it has always given me."

64. "I am grateful for all the times money has brought ease and peace to my life."

65. "Thank you, money, for being a reliable source of support and abundance."

66. "I am now open to receiving you, money, with joy and a sense of adventure."

67. "I am thankful for the role money has played in helping me achieve my dreams."

68. "I release all past resentments towards money and allow it to flow into my life with ease and appreciation."

69. "I understand that my negative views of money were unhelpful, and I now choose to treat money with gratitude and care."

70. "I consciously replace my past criticisms of money with a mature appreciation for its role in building a secure, fulfilling life."

71. "Money, you've made life easier and more joyful, and I know we'll keep doing amazing things together."

72. "I release any negative beliefs I've held about money and now welcome it with respect and gratitude."

73. "Money, you are my invitation to move toward the goals I've been waiting to pursue."

74. "Money, I appreciate how you've empowered me to explore, grow, and take new chances."

75. "I apologize for the ways I have misunderstood and undervalued money, and I now embrace it with appreciation."

76. "I honor the role money plays in my life, recognizing its importance in creating stability and growth."

77. "Money flows into my life with the same ease that I breathe—no effort, only trust."

78. "I treat money with the care and respect it deserves, knowing it can bring positive opportunities into my life."

79. "I shift my perspective, understanding that money is a form of energy that flows where it is respected and appreciated."

80. "I am thankful for the presence of money in my life and commit to managing it with wisdom and care."

81. "I choose to let money support my sense of fun, knowing that abundance enhances the joy I experience."

82. "I no longer view money as something negative, but as a meaningful part of my life that supports my well-being and success."

83. "I release past misunderstandings about money and now welcome it as a positive force for growth and possibility."

84. "I embrace a new mindset, one that honors money as something valuable and worthy of my respect and appreciation."

85. "Money, we've had our ups and downs, but I'm ready to trust and nurture our bond going forward."

86. "I see money as a ticket to more fun-filled adventures, and I'm ready to explore them."

87. "Money, you're not just here for transactions—you're a key to unlocking new adventures, and I thank you for that."

88. "I respect money for the opportunities it provides, and I use it wisely and with integrity."

89. "I release any past negativity I've attached to money and choose to welcome it with a responsible and appreciative mindset."

90. "Money, you've been patient with me, and now I'm ready to walk this path with you in gratitude and harmony."

91. "I trust that money supports all the fun I wish to have, and I open myself to endless enjoyment."

92. "It's been a journey, money, and now I'm open to seeing you as the ally you've always been."

93. "I understand that money supports my ability to create and contribute positively to the world."

94. "I don't need to control you, money. You flow freely into my life, bringing blessings when I trust you."

95. "I no longer speak negatively about money, but instead, I appreciate its potential to support my goals and dreams."

96. "I respect the flow of money into my life and handle it with maturity, knowing it supports both my personal and professional well-being."

97. "Thank you, money, for giving me the resources to grow and evolve."

98. "I'm ready to use money to create fun experiences that uplift and inspire me."

99. "I release the belief that I must struggle or work tirelessly to deserve money."

100. "I appreciate the times money has supported me in ways I hadn't expected."

101. "Thank you, money, for always being there to support my well-being."

102. "Money and I are learning to dance together—sometimes fast, sometimes slow, but always in sync."

103. "I am grateful for all the ways money has shown up for me throughout my life."

104. "I appreciate the consistent support money has provided in my personal growth."

105. "Thank you, money, for being a constant source of help and comfort in my life."

106. "I am thankful for all the times money has given me the freedom to pursue my passions."

107. "I am grateful for the presence of money in my life, and I commit to nurturing a respectful relationship with it moving forward."

108. "Money, I used to take you for granted, but now I honor how much you've done for me."

109. "I now see money as an ally that helps me achieve my goals and contribute to the well-being of others."

110. "I treat money with dignity, understanding that it reflects my ability to make responsible choices."

111. "I trust that money supports my desire to live a fun, carefree, and joyful life."

112. "You've opened paths for me that I didn't see, money, and I'm thankful for the journey you've helped me travel."

113. "I respect the role money plays in creating a balanced and secure life, and I use it wisely and thoughtfully."

114. "I acknowledge money as a valuable part of life, and I handle it with the care it deserves."

115. "I recognize that money reflects the energy and effort I put into the world, and I treat it with appreciation."

116. "I approach my financial decisions with maturity, ensuring that my actions reflect respect for the resources I have."

117. "I release any past judgments about money and now welcome it with a new, balanced understanding."

118. "I am grateful for the ways money supports my needs, and I commit to managing it responsibly and with respect."

119. "I've learned to appreciate you, money, not just for what you bring, but for how you allow me to be more of myself."

120. "I'm ready to work with you, money, as my ally, to create a life full of joy, purpose, and abundance."

121. "Money loves fun, and together we create a life full of laughter, adventure, and good times."

122. "I release any past disregard for money and now honor it as a meaningful part of my journey."

123. "I recognize money as an important resource and treat it with the respect and care it deserves."

124. "I value the presence of money in my life and handle it with thoughtful attention and maturity."

125. "I approach money with a balanced perspective, understanding its role in supporting my well-being and future."

126. "I respect the value of money, knowing it helps me create security and provide for my needs and goals."

127. "I'm done playing hide and seek with you, money—let's stay in sight of each other from now on."

128. "Money, I used to keep my distance, but now I'm inviting you into my inner circle where you belong."

129. "I treat money as something of value, and I make financial decisions that reflect my respect for its importance."

130. "I acknowledge money as a resource that, when respected and managed well, helps me build a stable, fulfilling life."

131. "I appreciate the role money plays in allowing me to pursue my dreams, and I commit to using it responsibly and gratefully."

132. "It's time for us to start fresh, money, where we can build something strong and positive without any past baggage."

133. "I welcome money as a key to unlocking more fun-filled opportunities and experiences."

134. "Money, I'm done worrying about you—I'm ready to trust that you'll come when I need you."

135. "I am grateful for the stability and comfort money has brought into my life."

136. "Thank you, money, for being a reliable source of support throughout my journey."

137. "I appreciate the ways money has allowed me to live a life of purpose and fulfillment."

138. "Thank you, money, for showing up for me and helping me build a secure future."

139. "I am grateful for all the ways money has been there to support my path forward."

140. "I appreciate the comfort and security money has provided me throughout the years."

141. "I invite money into my life in ways that feel light, free, and without strain, building a peaceful relationship."

142. "I appreciate how money has allowed me to experience joy and fulfillment."

143. "Thank you, money, for supporting me in every step of my personal and professional journey."

144. "I honor the flow of money in my life, treating it with respect and care."

145. "Money and fun are best friends in my world, always coming together to create new possibilities."

146. "Money, I'm ready to treat you with care and appreciation, without the fear that you'll leave."

147. "I am mindful of how I handle money, understanding its significance in my life."

148. "I welcome money with gratitude, knowing it helps me fulfill my responsibilities."

149. "I treat money with the respect it deserves, understanding its role in providing comfort and security."

150. "I manage my finances with maturity, ensuring I use money wisely."

151. "I appreciate the presence of money in my life and commit to honoring its value."

152. "I respect money's ability to help me create a life of balance and fulfillment."

153. "I understand the importance of money and handle it with thoughtful care."

154. "I'm ready to trust you, money, and stop worrying about where you'll come from next."

155. "I release any negative thoughts about money and replace them with respect and appreciation."

156. "I handle my finances with integrity, knowing that money supports my well-being."

157. "You and I, money, are finding a new rhythm, one that brings more peace and less stress."

158. "I'm letting go of my old habits with you, money, and I'm choosing to create healthier ones that last."

159. "I understand the value of money and make choices that reflect my respect for it."

160. "I've let go of the idea that I need to worry about you, money—I trust our relationship to flow naturally."

161. "Money, I'm ready to welcome you into my life without stress, creating a calm and steady connection."

162. "I welcome financial abundance into my life with respect, knowing it is a part of my growth."

163. "I manage my money with wisdom and maturity, ensuring it aligns with my values."

164. "I respect money's ability to provide for my needs, and I use it thoughtfully."

165. "Money is a tool that allows me to play, explore, and indulge in the joys of life."

166. "I approach my financial decisions with a calm and responsible mindset."

167. "I approach my finances with a healing mindset, finding joy in the flow rather than fear of the unknown."

168. "I release any past mistakes in handling money and now approach it with maturity and care."

169. "Money, I'm ready to take responsibility for how I manage you, knowing that responsibility creates freedom."

170. "You're not here to define me, money—you're here to give me options, and I appreciate that."

171. "I treat money with care, knowing it reflects the hard work and effort I put into my life."

172. "I respect money's potential to create positive change and manage it responsibly."

173. "I am grateful for how money has helped me meet my daily needs with ease."

174. "I appreciate how money has allowed me to make empowered choices in my life."

175. "Money flows to me through many channels, and I trust in the universe's generosity."

176. "Thank you, money, for providing me with the resources to manifest my dreams."

177. "Thank you, money, for supporting me as I work toward my life's purpose."

178. "I appreciate how money has allowed me to explore new possibilities with ease."

179. "Thank you, money, for giving me the freedom to pursue my passions and creativity."

180. "Money, I realize now that you reflect the energy I put out, and I'm ready to project abundance and calm."

181. "I am grateful for the opportunities money brings, and I handle it with care."

182. "I treat my financial resources with respect, ensuring they are managed well."

183. "You're no longer a mystery to me, money—I'm ready to learn, grow, and handle you with understanding."

184. "You're not something to hoard, money—you're meant to flow in and out, and I trust that process now."

185. "I'm choosing to be more thoughtful with you, money, knowing that when I honor you, you return that energy."

186. "I let go of stress around money and invite fun into our relationship, knowing joy leads to abundance.

187. "I release any negative beliefs about money and now see it as a source of potential and opportunity."

188. "I respect the flow of money in my life and commit to using it with wisdom."

189. "I treat money with the care and attention it deserves, knowing it supports my future."

190. "I deserve to receive money in all forms, including gifts, opportunities, and unexpected sources."

191. "You're not a prize to be won, money—you're a resource that makes life richer, and I'm ready to use you wisely."

192. "I release any unhealthy attachments to money and allow harmony and peace to guide our connection."

193. "I've stopped letting fear guide our relationship, money—now, I'm leading with gratitude and trust."

194. "Money, I see now that you're not about what I can get—you're about what I can create and share."

195. "I treat money as a valuable resource that supports my well-being and future success."

196. "I respect the role money plays in creating stability, and I handle it with care."

197. "I value the presence of money in my life and treat it with respect."

198. "I appreciate money for its ability to support my goals, and I manage it wisely."

199. "I've redefined success, money, and you're one of the tools I'm using to get there, not the destination itself."

200. "I approach financial decisions with care, knowing that money supports my path forward."

201. "I handle money with respect, knowing it plays an important role in my life."

202. "I'm no longer afraid of losing you, money—I trust that we have a natural ebb and flow, and I'm okay with that."

203. "You're no longer the thing I run after, money—you're the resource I invite in, knowing you'll support me."

204. "Money, I'm ready to use you in ways that benefit not just me, but the people around me, creating a ripple effect of abundance."

205. "Money, I've realized that you're not the answer to everything—but you do help me create the freedom to explore more, and I thank you for that."

206. "I've stopped worrying about where you come from, money—I trust that when I'm aligned, you show up in my life."

207. "Money comes to me with ease, and I allow myself to receive it without guilt or discomfort."

208. "Money, I don't need to force you into my life anymore—I'm open to letting you flow naturally."

209. "Money, I'm done making you the villain in my life—I see now that you're a tool for good when used mindfully."

210. "I treat money with care, appreciating the balance it brings into my life."

211. "I treat my finances with respect, knowing they contribute to my overall well-being."

212. "I treat money with respect, understanding its value in supporting my dreams."

213. "Money, I've learned that you aren't about survival anymore—you're about thriving, and I'm ready to thrive with you."

214. "I respect money for the freedom it provides and use it with care."

215. "Money, I'm ready to embrace you with an open heart, knowing you'll amplify the things that matter most to me."

216. "I treat money with the care and respect it deserves, knowing it supports my journey."

217. "I treat money with care, ensuring it reflects my commitment to a balanced life."

218. "Money, I've stopped treating you like something that comes and goes—I'm ready to build consistency with you."

219. "I'm learning that you, money, aren't about security alone—you're about creating the freedom to live fully and without limits."

220. "I forgive any past mistakes with money and choose to focus on healing and growth from this moment forward."

221. "Money, you're not just for paying bills—you're also for investing in experiences that matter to me."

222. "Receiving money without effort is a reminder that I am supported in all areas of my life."

223. "I've stopped fearing your absence, money—I know that when I live in alignment, you show up effortlessly."

224. "I approach money with gratitude, knowing it supports my path forward."

225. "I respect the value of money and manage it in a way that aligns with my long-term goals."

226. "Money, I'm ready to take you seriously, but without letting you take over my life."

227. "I've let go of the idea that you're hard to find, money—I'm open to the many ways you can come into my life."

228. "I am deeply grateful for all the times money has supported me."

229. "I appreciate the way money has provided for my needs and helped me thrive."

230. "Thank you, money, for supporting me in both big and small ways throughout my journey."

231. "Thank you, money, for giving me the freedom to make choices that align with my values."

232. "I am thankful for all the ways money has provided for my needs and desires."

233. "Thank you, money, for helping me navigate challenges with grace and ease."

234. "Money, I'm ready to be more mindful of how I use you, knowing that when I respect you, you grow."

235. "I am worthy of abundance whether it comes from effort or grace, and I welcome both."

236. "I am learning to view you, money, as a natural extension of my creative energy."

237. "Thank you, money, for providing for me in times of need and times of abundance."

238. "I am thankful for the role money has played in helping me create a life of stability, growth, and abundance."

239. "I choose to heal any emotional wounds I've tied to money, creating a path of harmony and abundance."

240. "Money, I'm letting go of any shame around you, allowing myself to enjoy what you bring into my life."

241. "Thank you, money, for providing me with opportunities to learn, grow, and expand."

242. "I am grateful for the times money has allowed me to experience new adventures."

243. "You're not something I need to conquer, money—you're an ally in my personal and spiritual growth."

244. "Thank you, money, for always being a source of comfort when I needed it."

245. "I trust that receiving money without struggle is part of my natural alignment with abundance."

246. "I appreciate the way money has given me access to education and personal development."

247. "Thank you, money, for allowing me to make my dreams a reality."

248. "I am thankful for how money has helped me overcome financial challenges."

249. "Thank you, money, for supporting my health and well-being."

250. "You're not a finite resource, money—you grow as I grow, responding to my openness and gratitude."

251. "Thank you, money, for the stability you've provided in times of uncertainty."

252. "I am grateful for the freedom money has given me to follow my passions."

253. "You help me share my gifts with the world, money, and for that, I honor our connection."

254. "Thank you, money, for being there when I've needed to invest in myself and my future."

255. "I appreciate how money has allowed me to create a peaceful and secure home."

256. "I welcome the support you offer, money, without needing to force or manipulate your arrival."

257. "Thank you, money, for supporting my ability to take care of my family."

258. "Thank you, money, for being a consistent force of stability and abundance."

259. "I appreciate how money has allowed me to give back to others and support those in need."

260. "Money, I release any doubts I've had about you and open myself to the abundance you bring."

261. "Thank you, money, for being there when I needed to invest in my happiness and growth."

262. "I am grateful for the way money has helped me take steps toward achieving my goals."

263. "It's okay for money to show up in my life unexpectedly, and I receive it with an open heart."

264. "I choose to let go of outdated beliefs about you, money, and welcome new ways of thinking."

265. "Thank you, money, for the opportunities you've given me to explore the world."

266. "I release past fears around money and trust that healing is taking place within our relationship."

267. "I appreciate the presence of money in my life, making it possible to live fully."

268. "Thank you, money, for being a reliable source of abundance, even in challenging times."

269. "You bring ease into my life, money, allowing me to focus on what truly matters."

270. "Thank you, money, for supporting me in building the life I've always dreamed of."

271. "I appreciate how money has helped me take care of my needs and aspirations."

272. "You are a vehicle for creating change, money, and I'm grateful for your role in my journey."

273. "Thank you, money, for allowing me to create meaningful experiences for myself and others."

274. "I am grateful for the peace of mind money has brought into my life."

275. "I release old limiting beliefs about money and open myself to a new chapter of healing and abundance."

276. "Thank you, money, for always showing up to help me build the life I desire."

277. "You are an amplifier, money, allowing me to magnify my intentions and make a greater impact."

278. "I appreciate how money has supported me in my spiritual growth."

279. "I release any shame around receiving money effortlessly and embrace the joy it brings."

280. "I am thankful for the sense of freedom and possibility money has brought into my life."

281. "I choose to allow more of you into my life, money, without needing to know exactly how."

282. "I am grateful for the opportunities money has given me to live a meaningful life."

283. "Thank you, money, for helping me build the foundation for a secure future."

284. "Money, I'm done with scarcity thinking—I now believe in your abundant flow into my life."

285. "I appreciate how money has allowed me to be generous with myself and others."

286. "I am thankful for all the financial support money has provided over the years."

287. "Money, I'm learning that you're not something to be earned with struggle—you're something to align with."

288. "Thank you, money, for making it possible for me to pursue the things I love."

289. "Thank you, money, for always providing what I need when I need it most."

290. "I am grateful for how money has allowed me to take care of my emotional and physical well-being."

291. "Money, I invite you to be a consistent presence in my life, without any stress or expectation."

292. "Thank you, money, for being a positive force that has helped me create the life I want."

293. "I appreciate how money has given me the ability to enjoy life's pleasures with ease."

294. "I forgive myself for any past mismanagement of money and open myself to a fresh, positive start."

295. "Money, I release any past fears that have blocked you, and I'm ready for a fresh start."

296. "I am thankful for the financial support money has offered during difficult times."

297. "Money, I no longer feel the need to compete for you—I trust that there is more than enough."

298. "I appreciate how money has provided me with access to experiences that expand my perspectives."

299. "I trust that I am worthy of receiving financial abundance in every form, without needing to earn it through labor."

300. "Thank you, money, for always being a dependable resource in my life."

Visualization Techniques

Healing Visualization Technique #1: Intergenerational Money Wound Healing

This visualization is designed to help you heal not only your current relationship with money but also to release any past financial wounds, including those carried from past lives, ancestors, and family members. It allows you to open yourself to higher truths and divine guidance, creating a new, healthy, and abundant relationship with money.

Step-by-Step Visualization:

1. **Set an Intention:** Begin by setting a clear intention to heal your relationship with money. You may say something like, "I invite my spirit team, higher self, and divine guidance to assist me in healing my past, present, and future relationship with money. I release all fears, anxieties, and negative beliefs

surrounding money and open myself to higher truths and abundance."

2. **Find a Comfortable Position:** Sit comfortably, either on a chair or on the floor, with your back straight and your feet grounded. Close your eyes, and take several deep breaths, inhaling through your nose and exhaling through your mouth, allowing yourself to relax.

3. **Open Your Chakras:** Visualize each of your chakras, from the base of your spine to the crown of your head. Imagine them opening up one by one, swirling with vibrant energy. See them as radiant and receptive to divine energy. Allow your chakras to be fully open, connecting you to both the earth and the universe.

4. **Receive Divine Energy:** Now, visualize divine energy pouring down from above, flowing through your open chakras, and moving through your arms into your hands. Feel this energy as a warm, radiant light, full of love, healing, and abundance.

5. **Create an Energy Ball:** With your eyes closed, bring your hands together in front of you, as if you are holding an invisible ball. Slowly begin to pull your hands apart, imagining that you are gathering divine energy between them. As you move your hands, feel the energy accumulating, forming into a powerful, glowing energy ball.

6. **Focus the Energy on Your Heart:** Once the energy ball feels strong and vibrant, bring it toward your heart. Visualize the energy radiating into your heart center, filling your entire being with healing light. As the energy works through your heart, it begins to heal your relationship with money, releasing any fears, worries, or negative patterns.

7. **Heal Past Versions and Ancestors:** As you hold the energy at your heart, say aloud or in your mind, "I heal my relationship with money. I heal my past versions, my ancestors, and my family's relationship with money." Visualize this energy radiating outward, healing not only your present self but also your past selves, your ancestors,

and your loved ones. See the energy flowing through time, clearing all financial wounds.

8. **Anchor Higher Truths:** As the healing energy continues to radiate through you, begin to anchor in higher truths. Say aloud, "I anchor higher truths about money. I welcome higher wisdom and understanding into my relationship with money." Feel this knowledge filling you, replacing old fears with love, trust, and abundance.

9. **Continue Until Complete:** Spend as much time as you need with this energy, allowing it to work through you until you feel complete. Let yourself be fully present with the process, releasing any emotions that arise. If you feel moved to cry or express emotions, allow them to flow—this is part of the healing.

10. **Close the Visualization:** Once you feel that the process is complete, gently bring your awareness back to the present moment. Close your chakras if you feel guided, imagining

them returning to a balanced state. Take a few deep breaths, grounding yourself back into your body and the present moment.

11. **Give Thanks:** End the visualization by thanking your spirit team, higher self, and the divine for guiding you through this healing process. Express gratitude for the healing that has taken place and for the higher truths you have anchored.

Why This Works:

This visualization works by healing the deep financial wounds you've inherited from both past experiences and your ancestral lineage. Through divine energy and heart-centered focus, you release old patterns of scarcity, fear, and limitations.

Healing Visualization Technique # 2:
The River of Abundance

This visualization is designed to help you tap into the natural flow of abundance and money in your life. By connecting with the imagery of a river, you will learn to let go of fear, anxiety, and control over money, and instead, trust in the infinite flow of abundance that is always available to you.

Step-by-Step Visualization:

1. **Set Your Intention:** Begin by setting an intention for this visualization. You might say something like, "I open myself to the natural flow of abundance. I release my fears around money and trust in the universe to support me."

2. **Find a Comfortable Position:** Sit or lie down in a comfortable position. Close your eyes and take a few deep breaths, allowing your body to relax fully.

Feel your feet firmly connected to the earth, grounding you in the present moment.

3. **Visualize a Calm, Flowing River:** Picture yourself standing beside a calm, flowing river. This river represents the energy of abundance, constantly flowing toward you and through your life. The water is clear, refreshing, and soothing, carrying with it all the resources, opportunities, and financial support you need.

4. **Release Resistance into the River:** As you stand beside this river, notice any feelings of fear, tension, or resistance you may have about money. Now, visualize these feelings as physical objects—perhaps rocks or debris—that you are holding in your hands. One by one, release these objects into the river, watching as they are carried away by the current. As you release each one, say aloud or in your mind, "I release my fear around money. I trust in the flow of abundance."

5. **Step into the River:** Once you have released all your resistance, take a step into the river. Feel the cool, refreshing water around your legs, gently supporting you as it flows. Allow yourself to relax into the feeling of being part of this infinite flow of abundance. Know that just as the river is always flowing, so too is the flow of money and prosperity in your life.

6. **Absorb the Energy of Abundance:** As you stand in the river, feel its energy surrounding you. Picture the water as shimmering with light, infused with the energy of abundance. Allow this energy to flow into your body through your feet and up through your entire being, filling every cell with the vibration of prosperity and peace.

7. **Receive and Give in Harmony:** Now, as you feel the energy of the river flowing through you, visualize yourself both receiving and giving. See money and resources coming to you effortlessly and see yourself using them wisely and kindly, sharing where needed.

Feel the balance between receiving and giving, knowing that you are part of this beautiful cycle of abundance.

8. **Anchor in Gratitude:** Spend a few moments standing in the river, feeling gratitude for all the abundance already present in your life. Say to yourself, "I am grateful for the abundance that flows to me effortlessly. I trust in the flow of prosperity."

9. **Step Out of the River:** When you are ready, step out of the river. Visualize yourself standing on the riverbank, feeling light, peaceful, and connected to the flow of abundance. Know that the river is always there, flowing, whether you are standing beside it or not. You are part of its energy, and it will always support you.

10. **End with Gratitude:** Take a few deep breaths and slowly bring your awareness back to the present moment. When you feel ready, open your eyes and give thanks for the healing and harmony you've experienced.

You might say, "I trust in the infinite flow of abundance. I am always supported."

Why This Works:

The river symbolizes the natural flow of abundance in life. By visualizing yourself letting go of financial fears and stepping into this flow, you invite peace and trust into your financial life. This visualization helps you shift from a mindset of scarcity or control into one of ease, trust, and alignment with the abundant energy of the universe.

Healing Visualization Technique #3:
The Tree of Abundance

This visualization is designed to ground you in the present moment while helping you connect with your inner source of abundance. Through the symbolism of a tree, you'll learn to root yourself in trust and strength, while allowing abundance to flow freely into your life.

Step-by-Step Visualization:

1. **Set Your Intention:** Start by setting your intention for the practice. You may say something like, "I open myself to the abundance within and around me. I release all limitations and trust in my natural ability to attract and receive wealth."

2. **Find a Quiet, Comfortable Space:** Sit or lie down comfortably. Close your eyes and take several deep breaths,

inhaling deeply through your nose and exhaling slowly through your mouth. Allow your body to fully relax.

3. **Visualize a Majestic Tree:** Now, imagine yourself standing in front of a large, beautiful tree. This tree is ancient, strong, and full of life. Its roots run deep into the earth, and its branches reach high into the sky. The tree symbolizes your deep connection to abundance, strength, and the infinite resources of the universe.

4. **Ground Yourself in the Earth:** Picture your feet sinking into the earth, just like the tree's roots. Feel the earth supporting you, grounding you, and nourishing you. As your roots sink deeper into the soil, feel a sense of stability and security. You are firmly grounded, knowing that you are supported by the universe in every moment.

5. **Draw Energy from the Earth:** With each breath, visualize the energy of the earth flowing up through your roots and into your body. This energy is abundant, nourishing, and

filled with life. As it flows into you, feel your body filling with strength, vitality, and abundance. This energy supports you financially, emotionally, and spiritually.

6. **Connect with the Tree's Wisdom:** Now, focus on the tree itself. Its branches stretch far and wide, bearing fruits and leaves that represent the infinite abundance available to you. The tree is wise, and its strength and wisdom are available to you. Ask the tree for guidance on your financial journey. Be open to any messages, symbols, or feelings that come to you.

7. **Visualize Abundant Fruits:** As you connect with the tree, visualize its branches heavy with fruit. Each fruit represents a form of abundance in your life—money, opportunities, support, or wisdom. See the fruit glowing with vibrant energy. Reach out and pick one of the fruits, knowing it is a gift from the universe, symbolizing the financial blessings flowing into your life.

8. **Receive the Gift of Abundance:** Hold the fruit in your hands and feel its energy radiating into your body. As you hold it, repeat to yourself, "I receive the abundance of the universe with gratitude and trust." Imagine this fruit dissolving into your hands, filling your entire body with the energy of abundance.

9. **Share and Spread Abundance:** As you absorb this energy, feel the abundance overflow from you. Just like the tree continues to grow and give, visualize yourself sharing this abundance with others—whether through acts of kindness, financial support, or simply radiating positive energy. Know that as you give, more abundance flows back to you in an endless cycle.

10. **Return to the Present Moment:** When you feel ready, take a deep breath and slowly bring your awareness back to the present moment. Picture the tree remaining in your heart, a symbol of your connection to infinite abundance.

Know that you can return to this tree whenever you need guidance or support on your financial journey.

11. **Express Gratitude:** Before opening your eyes, take a moment to express gratitude. Say to yourself, "I am deeply grateful for the abundance that flows into my life. I trust in the support of the universe." When you are ready, open your eyes and carry this feeling of abundance with you into your day.

Why This Works:

The tree is a powerful symbol of growth, stability, and abundance. By visualizing yourself connected to this tree, you ground yourself in the present moment and align with the natural flow of abundance. This visualization helps you recognize that abundance is not something external to be chased—it's already within you, always growing and ready to be received.

Healing Visualization Technique #4:
Rewriting Your Money Story

This visualization focuses on recognizing and rewriting the financial stories and beliefs you've held onto, allowing you to consciously create a new, positive narrative about money. This technique helps you shift from old, limiting patterns to a new, empowering relationship with money.

Step-by-Step Visualization:

1. **Set Your Intention:** Begin by setting an intention to release your old money stories and create a new, empowered narrative about wealth. You might say, "I am ready to release old financial patterns and create a new, respectful, and wise story about money."

2. **Find a Quiet, Comfortable Space:** Sit or lie down in a comfortable position. Close your eyes and take a few deep breaths, relaxing your body and clearing your mind.

3. **Visualize an Open Book:** Now, picture a large, open book in front of you. This book contains the story of your relationship with money, from your earliest memories to the present moment. The pages of the book represent the financial beliefs, experiences, and lessons you've accumulated throughout your life. Some pages may be positive, others may represent struggles or limiting beliefs.

4. **Review the Old Story:** Begin to scan through the pages of this book. As you do, notice the old financial stories you've carried. These might include beliefs like "Money is hard to come by," or "I'm not good with money." Allow these stories to surface, but do so without judgment. Simply observe the old patterns and beliefs that have shaped your financial journey.

5. **Release the Old Story:** As you reach the end of the book, imagine the last page being turned. Now, picture the book gently closing, and with it, the old financial stories are being released.

As you close the book, say to yourself, "I release all old beliefs and patterns around money. They no longer serve me."

6. **Visualize a New Blank Book:** After closing the old book, a new book appears before you—completely blank, with pure white pages. This new book represents your fresh start with money. You are free to write a new story, one based on respect, gratitude, maturity, and wisdom.

7. **Begin Writing Your New Money Story:** Visualize yourself picking up a golden pen and writing the first lines in this new book. As you write, focus on the financial life you want to create. You might write affirmations like, "I have a healthy, respectful relationship with money," or "Money flows to me easily, and I use it with gratitude and care."

8. **Anchor in Positive Beliefs:** As you continue to write, anchor in positive beliefs about money. Write statements like, "I trust in my ability to manage money wisely," or

"I am grateful for the financial support the universe provides." See yourself filling the pages with affirmations and intentions that align with your new, empowered relationship with money.

9. **Visualize Your Future Financial Self:** Now, imagine yourself years into the future, living out the financial story you've just written. Picture yourself feeling abundant, wise, and grateful for the wealth that flows into your life. Visualize yourself making empowered decisions with money, feeling completely at peace and aligned with your financial truth.

10. **Close the Book:** Once you feel complete, close the new book, knowing that your new money story is now written and will guide you forward. Say to yourself, "I trust in my new financial story. I am aligned with abundance and wisdom."

11. **Express Gratitude:** Before returning to the present, take a moment to express gratitude for the healing and transformation you've experienced. You might say, "I am grateful for the new story I've written. I trust in my ability to create a prosperous, respectful relationship with money."

12. **Return to the Present Moment:** Slowly bring your awareness back to the present moment. Take a few deep breaths, and when you're ready, open your eyes, knowing that you have created a new, empowering financial narrative.

Why This Works:

This visualization helps you consciously reflect on and release old financial stories while allowing you to create a new, empowering narrative about money. By writing this new story, you are taking control of your relationship with wealth and intentionally shaping a future based on respect, gratitude, and wisdom.

Healing Visualization Technique # 5:
Planting the Seeds of Financial Abundance

This visualization focuses on planting new intentions for financial growth and healing, just like planting seeds in fertile soil. By visualizing your financial goals as seeds that you nurture and care for, you develop a relationship with money that is based on patience, respect, and trust in the natural process of growth.

Step-by-Step Visualization:

1. **Set Your Intention:** Start by setting a clear intention. You can say something like, "I am ready to plant the seeds of financial abundance, healing, and growth. I trust in the natural flow of prosperity in my life."

2. **Find a Quiet, Comfortable Space:** Sit or lie down in a comfortable position, close your eyes, and take several deep

breaths. Let your body and mind relax, releasing any tension or financial worries.

3. **Visualize a Peaceful Garden:** Imagine yourself standing in a peaceful garden. The soil beneath your feet is rich, fertile, and ready to support new growth. This garden represents your financial life—a place where you will plant new seeds of abundance, healing, and wisdom.

4. **Hold Seeds in Your Hands:** Visualize yourself holding a handful of seeds in your hands. Each seed represents a financial intention, belief, or goal. These could be intentions like "I cultivate a respectful relationship with money," or "I am open to receiving financial support from the universe." Feel the weight of these seeds in your hands, knowing that they hold the potential for growth.

5. **Plant Your Seeds:** One by one, begin planting your seeds in the fertile soil of the garden. As you place each seed in the ground, state your financial intention aloud or in your mind.

For example, "I plant the seed of financial abundance," or "I plant the seed of gratitude and respect for money." Visualize each seed settling into the soil, knowing it will take root and grow.

6. **Nurture Your Seeds:** After planting the seeds, visualize yourself caring for them. See yourself gently watering the seeds, allowing sunlight to shine down, and creating the ideal conditions for growth. As you nurture the seeds, repeat to yourself, "I trust in the process of financial growth. I am patient, respectful, and grateful for the abundance that is growing in my life."

7. **Visualize Growth:** Over time, visualize the seeds beginning to sprout. See the first signs of growth breaking through the soil, symbolizing the financial changes and abundance beginning to manifest in your life. Feel a sense of trust in this process, knowing that as you continue to care for these seeds, they will grow into strong, healthy plants representing your financial goals.

8. **See Your Garden Flourish:** Now, fast forward in time and imagine your garden in full bloom. The seeds you planted have grown into beautiful plants, each one representing the abundance, wisdom, and respect you now have in your financial life. Visualize yourself walking through the garden, admiring the growth and feeling a deep sense of peace and gratitude for the financial abundance in your life.

9. **Anchor in Patience and Trust:** As you walk through the garden, anchor in the energy of patience and trust. Remind yourself that financial growth, like any form of growth, takes time and care. Say to yourself, "I trust in the natural flow of abundance. I am patient, and I nurture my relationship with money with respect and care."

10. **Express Gratitude:** Before leaving the garden, take a moment to express gratitude. Say, "I am grateful for the abundance that is growing in my life. I trust in the process and nurture my financial life with love and respect."

11. **Return to the Present Moment:** Slowly bring your awareness back to your surroundings. Take a few deep breaths, knowing that the seeds of abundance you've planted will continue to grow and thrive in your life. When you're ready, open your eyes and carry this sense of trust and patience with you into your financial decisions.

Why This Works:

This visualization emphasizes the process of growth, patience, and nurturing in your relationship with money. By visualizing your financial goals as seeds that need care and time to grow, you develop a respectful, wise, and patient relationship with money. This aligns with the idea that abundance, like any form of growth, requires attention, trust, and gratitude.

Healing Visualization Technique #6:
The Financial Compass of Wisdom

This visualization focuses on discovering and following your internal compass of financial wisdom. It helps you align your decisions and relationship with money toward respect, gratitude, and wise choices, guiding you to navigate your financial journey with confidence and clarity.

Step-by-Step Visualization:

1. **Set Your Intention:** Begin by setting a clear intention for this exercise. You might say, "I connect with my inner wisdom to guide my financial life with respect, clarity, and gratitude."

2. **Find a Comfortable Space:** Sit in a comfortable position with your feet firmly grounded, close your eyes, and take

several deep breaths, allowing your body and mind to relax completely. Let go of any stress or tension.

3. **Visualize a Calm, Open Space:** Imagine yourself standing in a peaceful, open landscape. The sky is clear, the air is fresh, and you feel calm and centered. This open space represents clarity and openness in your financial journey. In this space, you are free from distractions and external influences.

4. **See a Golden Compass in Your Hands:** Now, visualize a golden compass appearing in your hands. This compass represents your internal guidance system—your financial wisdom, intuition, and connection to higher truths about money. Feel the weight of the compass in your hands, knowing that it holds the power to guide you toward financial harmony.

5. **Set the Compass with Your Financial Intentions:** Gently hold the compass, and as you do, set clear intentions for your

financial life. These might include "I make wise, respectful decisions about money," or "I align my financial life with abundance and gratitude." As you set each intention, visualize the compass aligning itself with these goals, tuning itself to the direction of financial wisdom.

6. **Ask the Compass for Guidance:** Now, ask the compass to guide you toward financial decisions and beliefs that are aligned with respect, gratitude, and wisdom. You can say, "Show me the path to a respectful and wise relationship with money." See the compass needle pointing in a clear direction, representing your next steps or the financial truths you need to embrace.

7. **Receive Insights from Your Inner Wisdom:** Take a moment to receive any messages or insights from the compass. These could come as words, symbols, or feelings that offer guidance on how to harmonize your relationship with money. Trust that your inner wisdom is showing you the way toward financial peace and clarity.

8. **Visualize Walking the Path:** As the compass points in a clear direction, visualize yourself walking along that path. See yourself making wise, respectful financial decisions, feeling confident in your ability to manage money with maturity and gratitude. You are guided by your inner compass, always knowing which decisions align with your highest good.

9. **Anchor Financial Wisdom:** As you continue walking, anchor the feeling of financial wisdom within yourself. Say to yourself, "I trust my inner compass to guide me to financial harmony. I make decisions with respect, wisdom, and gratitude." Feel the sense of calm and clarity growing stronger with each step you take.

10. **Return to the Present with the Compass:** After walking the path, return to the open landscape where you began. The compass remains in your hands, symbolizing that you always have access to your inner financial wisdom.

Whenever you need guidance, trust that this compass is available to help you make wise, aligned financial choices.

11. **Express Gratitude:** Take a moment to thank your inner wisdom and the guidance you've received. Say, "I am grateful for the wisdom that guides me in my financial life. I trust in my ability to make wise and respectful choices." Feel the sense of peace and clarity staying with you.

12. **Return to the Present Moment:** Slowly bring your awareness back to your physical surroundings. Take a few deep breaths, and when you're ready, open your eyes. Carry this sense of guidance and confidence with you as you navigate your financial decisions moving forward.

Why This Works:

This visualization emphasizes connecting with your inner wisdom, represented by the compass, to guide your financial journey. It reinforces the idea that within you lies the ability to make mature, respectful, and wise financial choices. By trusting your internal compass, you align with clarity and confidence in your relationship with money.

Healing Visualization Technique #7:

The Vault of Infinite Abundance

This visualization invites you to connect with the concept of infinite abundance while releasing any fears or limiting beliefs surrounding money. By visualizing an abundant vault that is always accessible, you'll shift from a scarcity mindset to one of trust and respect for the flow of wealth.

Step-by-Step Visualization:

1. **Set Your Intention:** Start by setting an intention to connect with the infinite flow of abundance. Say to yourself, "I open myself to the infinite abundance of the universe. I release all fears and limiting beliefs about money."

2. **Find a Quiet, Comfortable Space:** Sit or lie down in a quiet space where you feel relaxed.

Close your eyes and take several deep breaths, allowing your body to relax completely. Let go of any tension or financial stress.

3. **Visualize a Grand Vault:** Imagine standing in front of a grand, secure vault. This vault represents the infinite flow of wealth and abundance available to you from the universe. It is not locked or guarded, but open and accessible, waiting for you to explore. Know that this vault contains everything you need—financial support, opportunities, and wisdom.

4. **Enter the Vault:** Visualize yourself stepping inside the vault. As you enter, you are greeted with an incredible sense of peace and security. The walls are lined with gold, jewels, and treasures that symbolize financial prosperity and abundance. You feel calm, knowing that this wealth is meant for you and is always available.

5. **Acknowledge Limiting Beliefs:** As you walk through the vault, take a moment to acknowledge any limiting beliefs or

fears you've held about money. These could be thoughts like "There's never enough," or "Money is hard to come by." Visualize these beliefs as small, old locks or chains lying on the floor of the vault. They are no longer needed, and they do not control your access to abundance.

6. **Release Limiting Beliefs:** One by one, visualize yourself picking up these old locks and chains. Gently place them in a small box, symbolizing your willingness to let them go. As you do, say, "I release all limiting beliefs about money. I trust in the infinite flow of abundance." See the box dissolving in the light, and with it, any financial fears or doubts are dissolved as well.

7. **Open Yourself to Abundance:** Now, focus on the treasures inside the vault. Each treasure represents a form of abundance you wish to invite into your life—whether it's financial stability, opportunities, or a healthy relationship with money. Reach out and hold one of these treasures in your hands, feeling its energy.

Say to yourself, "I am worthy of receiving this abundance. I welcome financial prosperity with gratitude and respect."

8. **Visualize the Flow of Abundance:** As you hold the treasure, visualize the vault's energy radiating outwards, flowing into your heart, mind, and entire being. This energy represents the flow of abundance in your life. Feel this energy dissolve any remaining financial tension or worry, filling you with peace and trust. Know that this flow is infinite and always accessible.

9. **Anchor Your Connection to Abundance:** As you continue to absorb the energy of the vault, anchor this connection to abundance. Say to yourself, "I am connected to infinite abundance. I trust in the flow of wealth and use it wisely and respectfully." Feel the truth of this statement resonate within you, anchoring a new belief in your financial life.

10. **Exit the Vault with Gratitude:** When you are ready, visualize yourself leaving the vault, but know that the energy

of abundance stays with you. This vault is always available to you whenever you need to access it. As you exit, say, "I am grateful for the infinite abundance that supports me. I trust in the universe to provide for me."

11. **Return to the Present Moment:** Slowly bring your awareness back to the present moment. Take a few deep breaths, and when you're ready, open your eyes. Carry this sense of connection to abundance with you, knowing that you are always supported financially.

Why This Works:

The vault symbolizes the infinite, accessible flow of wealth and abundance. By visualizing yourself stepping into the vault, you release limiting beliefs about money and invite a deeper trust in the universe's ability to support you financially. This visualization helps cultivate a respectful, wise, and peaceful relationship with money.

Conclusion

As you turn the last page of *Thank You, Money*, remember that this is not the end—it's a powerful new beginning. You've taken the first steps to heal and transform your relationship with money, shifting from tension and fear to gratitude, respect, and flow. The affirmations and visualizations within this book are tools designed to awaken your inner abundance and realign your mindset toward wealth with ease and joy.

This journey doesn't stop here. Money is energy, and like all energy, it responds to how you nurture it. You now have the power to continue evolving your relationship with money in ways that feel aligned with your highest self. Keep returning to these practices whenever you need to re-center, refocus, or recalibrate your money energy. This is a process, not a one-time fix, but with each practice, you are opening yourself to new possibilities, more wealth, and a deeper sense of peace.

Look at this moment as a fresh start—an opportunity to co-create your financial reality with the universe. Trust that by anchoring yourself in gratitude, releasing old beliefs, and inviting abundance into your life, you are setting the stage for a new chapter full of opportunities, financial flow, and unshakable peace.

Keep your heart open, your energy aligned, and know that you deserve the financial harmony that is already on its way to you. The road ahead is one of abundance, ease, and freedom—embrace it fully.

Thank you for allowing this book to be a part of your journey. Here's to a future filled with prosperity, joy, and endless possibilities.

About the Author

Sapphire Celestina is a passionate advocate for personal transformation and spiritual growth. With a deep interest in the interconnectedness of energy, abundance, and mindset, Sapphire blends practical wisdom with spiritual insight to help readers reshape their relationship with money. Her journey of healing her own financial mindset inspired her to create *Thank You, Money: Affirmations to Heal and Harmonize Your Relationship with Money*, a guide for those ready to release limiting beliefs and embrace abundance with gratitude and ease.

Through her work, Sapphire encourages others to approach money from a place of respect, trust, and alignment with their highest selves. She believes that money, like any other form of energy, can flow freely and easily when treated with care, and her affirmations and visualizations are designed to facilitate this transformation. When she's not writing, Sapphire enjoys creating art, exploring the mysteries of consciousness, and helping others on their spiritual journeys.

Other Works by Sapphire Celestina

In addition to *Thank You, Money*, Sapphire Celestina is also the author of *Beyond Wealth: Exploring the Spiritual Truths That Transcend Money*. *Beyond Wealth* is a journey into the spiritual aspects of abundance, inviting readers to explore the truths that go beyond material wealth. It complements *Thank You, Money* by helping you understand the deeper, spiritual principles that guide abundance and prosperity.

While *Thank You, Money* provides affirmations and visualizations to help you shift your financial mindset on a practical level, *Beyond Wealth* opens the door to higher spiritual wisdom, allowing you to see wealth in a broader, more profound context.

By understanding both the practical and spiritual aspects, you create a holistic relationship with wealth. Together, these books offer a powerful blend of insight. Reading both of these works creates a complete journey of financial and spiritual transformation, helping you align with abundance in every form.

www.ingramcontent.com/pod-product-compliance
Lightning Source LLC
Chambersburg PA
CBHW062116220526
45471CB00010B/3750